I0468542

Becoming Harvey Specter: Get the Job, Style, Knowledge and Lifestyle, and Live Life Like Harvey Specter

LEE BURR

For my Mike Ross.

CONTENTS

ACKNOWLEDGMENTS

Suits, Harvey Specter, and just about every other reference in this book are trademarks of USA Network. Without them, there would be no Suits, and thus, no book. The show is great, and this book isn't intended to breach any rights, trademarks or laws. I'm sure USA Network's lawyers are awesome and understand, just like you do, that this book is intended to inform, educate, and express opinions, which incidentally is protected under the First Amendment to the U.S. Constitution.

1 HOW HARVEY WAS BORN

Somebody once told me to write for the person that hasn't got a clue what you're talking about. With that being said, I will now briefly explain *Suits* and Gabriel Macht, the actor who plays Harvey Specter in the show, to my mother. Quite why I'm doing this I've yet to figure out, as who would really buy a book about becoming a guy they've never heard of? In fact, I'm rather tempted to exclude this section from the book, just so they continue to have no idea what the show is about. But that would be mean. Very mean. And I'm not that kind of guy.

About Harvey Specter

Jessica Pearson came across Harvey when he was doing a job in the mailroom at Gordon Schmidt Van Dyke.

In the mailroom, Harvey realized that an associate had knowingly dated a postage wrong as he had missed the filing. He came to Jessica's office to report this misconduct and said that if she did not report this misconduct, then he would to the DA. Jessica was impressed by Harvey's eye for law and courage. She sent Harvey to Harvard Law School where he met Dana Scott, his rival and also his lover on and off.

Harvey graduated 5th at Harvard Law School and then Jessica sent him for "trial experience" to work under the New York District Attorney Cameron Dennis. She wanted Cameron to be the only one Harvey should learn from. Hence, Harvey worked as an Assistant District Attorney (ADA) under the leadership of Cameron for 2 years. It is there that he met Donna Paulsen, who he hired as his secretary and also became one of his most trusted advisor, friend and colleague. Harvey caught Cameron destroying and hiding proof on his cases and hence, decided to leave him. He seeked a job at Pearson Hardman and took Donna with him as his secretary. He was hired at Pearson Hardman as a sophomore associate but very quickly climbed up the ladder to become a senior associate. He met Zoe Lawford at Pearson Hardman, an associate with whom Harvey had a shared attraction with.

In the year 2007, Jessica approached Harvey with a serious problem of money being embezzled from Pearson Hardman. Initially, a junior partner, Louis Litt was suspected but Jessica and Harvey later realized it was actually Daniel Hardman, the other managing partner doing the embezzling. With the help of Donna, Jessica and

Harvey discover that Daniel is cheating the firm and stealing money from it to splurge on Monica Eton, the lady who he is having an extramarital affair with. They blackmail Hardman to surrender his seat to Jessica. This also leads Harvey to being promoted to a junior partner. Harvey occasionally visits his father's grave and shares drinks with his grave. His office also holds a record of his father, who played the saxophone.

The show starts off with Harvey finally becoming the senior partner, his life-long dream. He needs to appoint an associate who graduated from Harvard. Harvey selects Mike Ross, a very intelligent young man but with a troubled past, who is involved in some illegal activities but still looking to get his break in law. Mike Ross has never really graduated from any law school but still knows the law back and forth. Harvey is very impressed with Mike Ross's picture perfect knowledge of Law and his intelligence and agrees to take on the risk of keeping Mike's secret safe. Harvey takes on Mike to assist him with many cases and together they make a great team. Mike and Harvey have many similar traits. Harvey is often shown helping those in unfavourable situations and helps the ones he knows, even if it means risking his own reputation.

Season 2 starts off with Harvey facing a conflict with the managing partner and also his friend, Jessica Pearson learning the bitter reality about Mike. Moreover, Harvey also has to assist Jessica in handling the come back of Pearson Hardman's second managing partner, Daniel Hardman whom both Jessica and Harvey do not trust. Harvey is clearly looking out in Jessica's best interests and

Hardman's return causes sparks to fly between Hardman and Harvey.

Harvey and Jessica work closely together to keep the problems hidden from Hardman. The season shows flashbacks of both Mike and Harvey and how their past decisions have moulded their present. Harvey's closer skills are needed more and more by Jessica to keep the chaos from Daniel as well as to throw him out as a partner. The episode Blood in the Water shows Harvey coming to the rescue of the firm again which is now rid of Daniel Hardman but faced with a new crisis. Harvey has to compete with Robert Zane, who is Rachel Zane's father on a gender prejudice case. In the finale of Season 2, Pearson Hardman agrees to a merger with a British company owned by Edward Darby. Harvey is not pleased with this merger as he does not have faith or trust in Edward.

The third season continues with Harvey as the senior partner and the firm merged as Pearson Darby. He is given a very high profile case by Darby of Ava Hessington. Harvey and Jessica work together on this case to get Ava free from all the charges. Meanwhile, Louis Litt takes Mike under his leadership saying that Harvey has nothing more to teach him. Harvey has to go all out in the case when Ava goes to prison for murder. Moreover, Darby's closer and "fixer" Stephen Huntley arrives to make things worse for Harvey. In the episode, "Shadow of a Doubt," Stephen and Harvey begin to work collectively on the case. Things are looking gloomy for Harvey with Cameron Dennis, the opposing counsel for the case trying all unofficial strategies to make Harvey lose. Harvey and Stephen get into an argument on how to tackle the case and the case goes to trial. However, Jessica and Mike are both doing their best along with Harvey to rescue the firm. Harvey discovers that the order to carry our murder actually came from Stephen Huntley as at that time, he was Ava Hessington's fixer. However, Edward Darby did not know of this. There is only one way left to rescue Ava Hessington from an assassination trial and that is for Jessica and Harvey to come up with a settlement offer for Cameron Dennis. In this settlement, Edward Darby will swear against Stephen Huntley asserting that Edward Darby knew about the murder orders.

Cameron has a standard of catching the right bad guys and he agrees to Harvey's proposal that Edward will testify against Stephen and Cameron will subsequently drop all charges against Ava. When the Settlement Agreement was being signed, Edward Darby realizes that there is one extra clause that prevents him from practicing his legal career in New York City. This was actually a plan derived by Jessica to throw out Edward from Pearson Darby. Edward Darby has no other option but to agree to the settlement as he has to protect his relationship with Ava Hessington as he shared a very close relationship with her father.

However, the trouble again stirs up in the firm when Ava Hessington employs Travis Tanner to charge Pearson Darby Specter for misconduct. Travis Tanner is a tough opposition and he proves it in the deposition with Harvey. Moreover, he is also playing dirty by involving Dana Scott into the picture to put Harvey on the defensive. In the deposition of Dana Scott, it is revealed that Stephen

Huntley had lied in his affidavit asserting that Dana Scott knew about the orders for the murder. Subsequently, Mike Ross and Donna Paulsen go to prison to confront Stephen Huntley on his affidavit. Stephen Huntley admits to Donna that he had lied in the affidavit. However, he forgot that all conversations are recorded in prison.

During the deposition of Ava Hessington by Harvey, Harvey goes off the record and apologizes to Ava Hessington but stays firm that whatever he had done was in Ava's best interest. Ava Hessington accepts Harvey's apology and Harvey makes fun of Travis Tanner.

In this season, Jessica Pearson finds out that Mike Ross and Rachel Zane are a couple. She forces Mike to get an affidavit signed by Rachel admitting that she has knowledge about Mike Ross' fake Harvard Degree. This implicates Rachel Zane as one of the employees of the firm who is backing up the cover up of Mike Ross's academic identity. Rachel Zane brings the affidavit back to Jessica Pearson but asks something in return if she signs it. She asks to be an employee of the firm after graduating from Columbia Law School and breaking the firm's legacy of only hiring Harvard Law graduates.

Relationships

Harvey is a brilliant, charming and persuasive man and lawyer, but his good side is not for everyone to see. His handsome looks, smile, confidence and charisma makes him popular with both ladies and his clients. He easily gets what and until he does not get it, he does not rest in peace. Not many people like him as they are often exposed to his mean, pompous side. Harvey's colleagues, especially Louis Litt share mixed feelings of admiration and resentment towards Harvey. Donna says that this is because no one likes that Harvey is right all the time. However, he surely deserves the admiration based on his thirst to always win, work ethics and unorthodox methods.

Harvey has few but very close and well-guarded personal relationships. He can use his wit and cold demeanour to keep people away as well as show his soft side and pull them towards him. Regarding trust, he either trusts people completely or not at all. There is no middle way for him as for him, relationships are black-and-white. On the exterior, Harvey shows his not caring side as he thinks showing too much care is a weakness for him as well as his job. However, due to this outlook, he has formed an impenetrable armour around himself whereby he refuses to show anyone his vulnerable side. Harvey, maybe due to his past regarding his mother has always kept himself emotionally distant from everyone and Louis mentions that he will always be alone. However, Harvey does express himself and voices his concern for those close to him like Mike, Donna and Jessica.

Jessica Pearson

Jessica Pearson is not only Harvey's boss but also his mentor, guide and a close friend. There is no doubt in her mind that Harvey is her "ace-in-the-hole," and her right-hand man at Pearson Hardman. She is sure that Harvey will always have her back. This trust has never been broken by Harvey as well. Jessica has "raised" Harvey with a silver spoon in his mouth. She and Harvey first met when he was working in the mailroom of Pearson-Hardman. Back then, Harvey was outraged that an associate has back-dated the postage for a missed filing and committed fraud. He threatened to go to the DA with this report of misconduct if Jessica did not do anything about it. Jessica instantly sensed potential and integrity in this man and put him through Harvard Law. After Harvey's graduation, she continued to guide his career and sent him to Cameron Dennis at the DA's office for trial experience. She believed that at this stage in his career, Harvey should only be learning from Cameron. After two years, she hired Harvey to work for her at Pearson Hardman and he went on to become senior partner for the firm. Harvey is the youngest senior partner at Pearson Hardman to be promoted.

Jessica likes and trusts Harvey because of his fiery lust for ambition, stubbornness, and loyalty. She believes that due to these traits of Harvey, Pearson Hardman is so successful. Jessica is more cautious about the risks she is willing to take, but Harvey is a "shoot-from-the-hip" kind of man. She is extremely lenient with Harvey as his unorthodox methods usually garner a win for the firm. Jessica's strong ruthless demeanour allows her to appreciate Harvey's ferocious need to win and she usually bends the rules for him. However, Harvey is not very happy when her orders contradict his strategy and this trait of his troubles her. However, there is still no doubt in her mind that Harvey is her "ace-in-the-hole,". Yet, she keeps a close eye on him at all times.

Harvey and Jessica share the playful banter of two close friends. They might not agree on everything, but they have a lot of respect for each other's wit and abilities, and are always loyal with each other. It is not possible that one will ever work without the other. Although you will never see them hugging, their relationship is very deep and powerful and together they make a power-packed team at Pearson Hardman.

2 LANDING THE JOB

"I don't pave the way for people... People pave the way for me"

We've broken the character of Harvey Specter down into little juicy, bite sized segments, now it's time to start putting it all back together. These next few chapters will look at what it is Harvey does, and ways we can mimic that to become someone that loosely resembles the man himself. Make sure you read the warnings at the end though. Seriously.

The Pros and Cons of Being a Lawyer

Harvey Specter is a top class lawyer. Arguably if you

want to be more like Harvey Specter, you need to be a lawyer. Before we dive in and say, that becoming a lawyer is the be all and end all of becoming more like Harvey Specter; lets take a look at the pros and cons of practising law and see if there's anything we can pick out from the practise that could be applied to other areas of work that you may enjoy more.

First of all, lawyers are paid well, there's no two ways about it. Successful attorneys will bring home an awful lot of money. On the flip side to that though, they also have to deal with a lot of stress, potentially some guilt, along with a sprinkling of alienation after years of dealing with some unsavoury characters and some tough cases.

Practising law can be exciting at times, for those who enjoy strategy, confrontation and a bit of drama. Becoming a lawyer can provide all of that and more. However, in order to get to that stage, there is an awful lot of reading through boring documents and files.

One of the reasons I considered law when I was looking at degrees, was the fact that law is varied. Every month you could be working on a different case, which involves different knowledge and working with different people. No two cases are ever going to be identical and as they say variety is the spice of life. It's worth pointing out that some types of law can involve similar cases though such as, property law.

One of the major downsides to becoming a lawyer though, is the stress that comes with it. Harvey Specter is constantly under a lot of stress and pressure to deliver. Whilst he sometimes palms a lot of work off on to Mike Ross, he doesn't shy away from long hours and hitting deadlines himself. Harvey's confidence is a major asset when it comes to law, because ultimately you can never be too certain that you're going to win and in some firms on some cases, not winning could cost you your job.

All in all, whether you think practising law is the right move for you, comes down to individual preference. Some people revel in the risks and stresses that go with those jobs; the deadlines and so on. This feeds the excitement and variety of the role further. Other people can certainly see the attraction in practising law. For me the variety each week of each case was attractive and the strategizing element of the job tempted me to look a bit closer, but for me the stresses and the strains that it would've put on my personal life, were too high; obviously not for Harvey Specter.

3 BUILDING THE KNOWLEDGE

"I don't play the odds, I play the man"

Harvey Spectre is a clever man. There is no two ways about it, so I guess if you want to 'become' Harvey, you're going to need to seriously up your game when it comes to your knowledge. I've broken this section down into two sections; learning and knowing. Whilst you might see both as the same thing, they are actually rather different. You can learn about Law, but still not no the sentence for a specific crime. Simple example, but it shows that there is a subtle, yet distinct difference.

How to Learn Anything in 20 Hours

The First 20 Hours by Josh Kaufman is a great book that details how to acquire skills quickly and easily. Effectively it proposes that you can learn anything within 20 hours. He calls it rapid skill acquisition, the skill and exercise of acquiring new abilities as quickly and effectively as you possibly can.

The main concept and theory put forward by Josh Kaufman is that with just a bit of careful planning and strategy, you can study almost anything and learn the basics to a sufficient level within around 20 hours of fast, concentrated, focused effort. And whilst 20 hours sounds like a lot, sometimes in fact more than frequently it is less. I can vouch personally for Josh Kaufman's theory that it works and that if you're looking to acquire a new skill, perhaps something that Harvey Specter is particularly good at, 20 hours can be all it takes. But what about if you wanted to be more like Harvey Specter in the fact that he's a world class lawyer an attorney. Well the theory put forward by Josh Kaufman is that all you need to do is actually learn twelve different skills to a satisfying level and there you have it, you're now an expert or you can class yourself as an expert within that over-arching field.

It's a book I thoroughly recommend reading if this is an area of Harvey Specter's life you want to take further. If you don't have the time or inclination, very briefly here it is summarised.

The first three sections of the book detail the most important concepts and theories. These are things such as the distinction between learning and practising. It also introduces two key lists, known as the ten concepts of rapid skill acquisition and the ten concepts of effective learning. All of these sections are motivating and Josh Kaufman manages to get you excited about learning. In fact if you were only toying with the idea about learning something before reading theses three sections, by the end of it you'll be rushing out, blocking out 20 hours of your time and putting your mind to work.

The six sections that follow, act as almost case studies. Josh Kaufman runs through six different skills that he learnt himself using this very method. All of these skills that Kaufman learnt, were acquired within 20 hours. Things such as yoga, touch typing, playing the ukulele, programming a web code and wind surfing. These are all things that can be learnt within just 20 hours according Kaufman. And whilst at times it does sound like Josh Kaufman is boasting just a little bit, it is also very helpful to read, to understand what the learning framework looks like when applied to real life situations.

I suppose the most important thing to take from the book, are the ideas of immersing your self within a skill, putting your total focus on to that at that moment in time, removing all distractions such as phone calls, internet if it's not required and other people in the room and focus purely on learning that skill.

Kaufman also highlights the fact that if your unsure whether you should dedicate 20 hours of your time to learning something new, then perhaps you should look for something else. He also highlights the fact that the quality of the skill that you practice is much more important than the quantity. By this he means, you shouldn't be rushing through 20 hours trying to get to a satisfactory standard before moving onto something else. If it does take you a little bit longer, stick with it. Don't just move onto the next thing and just forget about it ticking it off your checklist, ticking it off your bucket list. Once you've learnt a skill enjoy it and just like when you study for a PHD, if you start reading into a subject and learning about something and you find your self being drawn off on a tangent let your self go on that tangent. Of course don't count that in the 20 hours of work. By letting yourself read into and research the subject further, you'll not only become more interested in it, you'll also find some interesting sub skills that may be required should you want to be known as more of an expert within the field.

Ultimately Josh Kaufman breaks down the idea of skill acquisition into three distinctive stages. The first known as cognitive or the early stage of learning could be attributed to the things such as research and understanding and thinking about how certain elements of that skill can be broken down into workable and actionable parts. The second stage is associative or intermediate, these are things such as practising what you've learnt, acting on feedbacks acquired and changing the way you do things based on that feedback. The final stage of learning that Josh Kaufman details is autonomous also know as the late stage of learning. At this point, you know that you've acquired a new skill because you're able to carry it out with little to no thinking or attention.

If you think of this when you look...

If you think back to when you learnt how to drive a car, these three stages are easily identifiable. The first stage is learning where the pedals are and what they do, learning that the steering wheel alters the position of the wheels and allows you to drive round corners. The mirrors allow you to see behind and what is behind you; this is the cognitive stage.

The second stage, the intermediate stage or associative stage is when you start to apply those thoughts and theories and you start to move the steering wheel whilst driving. You put those elements into practice and you take on the feedback from your driving instructor.

Finally you've passed your driving test, you've been driving for a year or so and you're able to reach the biting point of the clutch on a manual car nice and easily or you're able to parallel park without too much effort. This is the autonomous stage; you're effectively able to complete the skill of driving without thinking.

If you want to be a bit more like Harvey Specter, apply Josh Kaufman's theory of the first 20 hours will allow you to get there in a lot less time than the standard ways of learning a new skill.

How to Know Anything in 30 Seconds

Understanding how to navigate the internet effectively is a vital skill, and you will find many different ways that you could discover the information you're searching for. Although the list below of tips and websites is in no way thorough, there is enough to enable you to get started in knowing anything in 30 seconds or less. The trick to all of this is, of course, Google.

Using Google Operator Hacks

Google allows you to search for more than just words. You can find books, images, locations, in fact, you name it, Google can probably help you find it. Unfortunately, Google is just a machine though, so in order to find what you're looking for, you need to be able to know how to search the database effectively and quickly. Google Search Operators allow you to do just that. Learn these, and with a smartphone in one hand, you'll be able to be just like Harvey Specter – know everything!

This is a choice of some of the most useful ones:

salsa -dance will discover pages that contains salsa although not dance

castle ~reference will discover pages that contains glossaries and terminology associated with castle

define:matador brings up definitions from the word matador

~crocodile will look for the term crocodile and other alike words

lon sfo to reserve plane tickets from London to Bay Area

delta flight 5778 to determine the status of the flight

love   site:world   wide

web.matadornetwork.com/existence to look only Matador Existence for that word love

love   -site:world   wide web.matadornetwork.com/existence to exclude Matador Existence is a result of your research for love

And remember if you wish to go to a site that's lower, or that the company's server won't allow you to access, you will see the Cached version to determine a Google snapshot of this page from the time it had been last indexed.

Further Online Investigation

Performing online investigation is all about not only typing a couple of words into Google, even when you need to do be aware of operator hacks! You will find lots of assets available that will help you. Heres how to locate:

Scriptural text: Find specific text in the Bible at BibleGateway.

Books Online: Google Books includes a surprising quantity of free books available on the web, and includes search features which are ideal for research. It is also worth looking at Project Gutenberg, that has freely available digital copies well over 33,000 formerly released game titles.

Proceedings: LexisNexis has a number of cases readily available for free.

Etymology: Discover the cause of any word at Etymoline.

Human Sources: Help a Reporter Out (HARO) is a great service that allows you interact with people all over the world who can provide you with information or quotes on subjects you're researching.

Newspapers: Newspapers dating back to 100s of years can be found in the Google News Archives, but you may also use LexisNexis if you have a regular membership or can login using a college network.

Primary Materials from around the globe: The UNESCO World Digital Library is really a digital compendium of great primary materials from nations and cultures all over the world.

Scholarly Sources: Google Scholar is really a compendium of 1000's of research articles.

And when you need to take advantage of the digital brain from the Internet, make use of the twitter search feature and look for typically the most popular Google Insight stats to determine exactly what the online population are planning on.

4 GETTING THE LIFESTYLE

"Sometimes good guys gotta do bad things to make the bad guys pay"

There are hundreds, if not thousands of books available on the subject of creating an 'ideal lifestyle', but not one of them focuses on creating a Harvey Specter lifestyle. That is what this section is all about, and whilst many of the ideas that I'll throw in to the mix are borrowed and developed from other authors and thinkers original work, these ideas are all about getting the lifestyle that most closely replicates that of Mr Specter. In case you've forgotten what that is, go back and read the chapter on how Harvey was born.

Culture Yourself

Harvey Specter is a man of culture, if you want to become Harvey Specter you need to learn how to culture yourself. Whether you are 16 or 60, in order to culture yourself you need to take part in the complex culture that is available in present day society. This section aims to teach you how to become more cultured, interesting and ultimately a more well rounded person on your own. Unfortunately this section will not culture you, rather it will teach you how to culture yourself.

Firstly, understanding what it means to be cultured. A cultured person could be somebody that is an eclectic reader, perhaps they watch well written, classic films, they might prefer the opera, or have a refined appreciation for art. To become cultured is another way of saying, to be educated concerning the world, its languages, its politics, its history and most importantly its art. A cultured individual is somebody that has an interest in culture and participates actively within it.

Most of modern culture originates from books, because they have been around for far longer than other forms of media. So therefore a quick way to become cultured is to read a lot of classic books, but when you start out as an uncultured person this can seem a bit daunting and rather unexciting. Instead select just one genre that you are genuinely interested in, for example you may choose fantasy or romantic fiction. Investigate what the best books and authors of the genre are, not judged by Amazon reviews but by book critics; well renowned book critics from within the industry. At the same time you might find yourself looking into other genres that appeal to you and as you read more and more books your tastes will evolve. Let this happen and if you find yourself moving from romance to science fiction that's perfectly acceptable and vice versa. Along with this, if there's a genre that you're not sure about, go and investigate for yourself. Once you feel you've become reasonably well read, within a single genre, it's time to move on and pick another. Try to pick out some classic books as well within the genres, not just the latest releases. Whilst the latest releases receive all of the marketing hype, they're often based around older classical stories.

Sign up for magazines and journals, which are centered around literature, plays and music. I'm not talking about NME or Kerrang, rather lifestyle magazines that offer insight into music of years gone by as well as more contemporary music that is perhaps, less well appreciated at the moment. Read articles from all of these magazines, once or twice a week or just when schedule allows. When you read something that you're interested in, follow it. Look up that music on Youtube or Spotify and every now and again, you'll find a piece of art, a play or a piece of music that you've never heard before, that you find yourself falling in love with. Should you read an article on a great artist or sculptor who sounds interesting, use the internet to discover, which museums feature their work and see if you can schedule in some time to go and view it. If money or time is tight, you can also scan your local newspaper for theatrical productions by local universities, schools and colleges that you could attend. Some of these productions can be just as eye opening as the professional production.

Being cultured is more than just reading though. Once you've absorbed that information and the culture around you, start writing. Everybody's able to write poetry, short tales, books or even plays. Being cultured means replying to culture not just absorbing it; and the easiest way of doing that is to make your own. It is possible just to comment on things that you see, music that you listen to and books that you read. However, sometimes it's easy to mix up discussion with argument around these things.

Modern day culture also encompasses films. Whilst it is crucial to read books, it's also vital that you watch films regularly. As with books, don't just look to the latest releases, in fact it's wise to sometimes avoid those. Instead look back on classic films from directors of years gone by. Look up their work, watch their back catalogue and find out what all the fuss is about with them. Appreciate their art, comment on it and reply to it. Once you've watched a film, go and read some reviews; these can be from magazines or online. They can be user published or they can be critical. Do you agree with them? When you read these reviews, they'll often comment on other pieces of work by the same director or actor. Go and investigate those and go and lose yourself in the web of films. Don't restrict yourself to just British language films either, there are a number of other available films worth watching in a variety of languages. Some of these can be just as eye opening and will help you culture yourself as any British film could do.

Television isn't something that immediately springs to mind when we think of culturing ourselves, however what television can do is allow you to, assess what the rest of the population is watching on a regular basis. Watch the news, but don't just listen, deconstruct, take notes if it helps, understand how the anchorman or woman holds the position of authority. Notice how stories are structured. Is bad news put first, followed by good news? Is good news put first, followed by bad news? How do they generally end a broadcast? This isn't just watching television programs, it is understanding them and understanding how they're put together and at that point you'll be able to understand how modern day media is feeding our culture and as such you can become more cultured yourself. Of course, there are some great television channels out there such as the discovery channel and the history channel. This can be a really easy method of getting involved with subjects like the roots of impressionist art or even the reputation for British people.

I've already touched on music a lot in this section and

there's good reason for that. Music encompasses so many elements of our culture, unfortunately though, so many people are narrow-minded when it comes to music, sticking to just one genre that they like. Music has come to define cultures; look at the rock scene and the metal scene, the glam rock scene, the punk rock scene, all variations on one main genre but have very distinct cultural ideologies.

The difference between an individual of one of those cultures and an individual of culture is that the individual of culture admires the niche music genres, they pick out the elements that they enjoy and rather than disrespecting the areas that they don't enjoy they choose to wash over them. Don't just stop at the genres that you've heard of perhaps don't like though, look at genres that you have never listened to before. An individual of culture will pay attention and revel in tunes with non-cliché lyrics; they will also look to music without lyrics at all. They'll listen with intent purely for the atmosphere it may set or even for the story it tells without words. Classical music is often seen as a daunting prospect for anyone who has not listened to it before; they don't know what they're meant to be listening to. The easiest way to start is to just listen, listen to some famous musical pieces and you'll realise why they are famous.

Furthermore, pay attention to albums as well, not just the main singles. Whilst the singles are often the catchy numbers and albums are quite legitimately just album fillers, there are also so hidden gems in there that you may discover.

Modern day culture isn't just about classical music and classic literature though; you can culture yourself by playing video games. Many people think it's a bit nerdy playing video games but is a culture in itself. The gaming culture has grown and grown and grown and now to truly class yourself as a cultured individual you should be able to hold a conversation with a gamer, understanding the difference between an RPG game and first person shooters.

Take part in internet culture; remember that classic culture was at some point present culture. Our present culture can be found online. The digital age that we live in is magnificent, so embrace it and rather than focusing purely on years gone by, get stuck in online, enjoy memes and viral videos and understand how gif's work. Set your homepage to Wikipedia and browse through different articles each day that you log online. Search for things that appear cultured to you, read the article, understand the article and in a very short amount of time you will be aware of a lot more things and a lot more cultures than you are at the moment.

Stepping back from the online realm though, art is something that to become cultured, you really have to embrace. It's often considered the most potent type of communication. Art crosses language borders and even cultural barriers for we all see things both differently and the same. The meaning we take from a piece of art can be different, however the painting that we're looking at is the same. View art on your computer, but also visit art galleries. Many art galleries are free, so there really is no excuse for not broadening your horizons.

Perhaps the best way to culture yourself though is through travel. It's an old cliché but travel really does broaden the mind. Rather than read about other cultures, or viewing videos of animals online. Why not go there and witness for yourself first hand. Travelling seeks to outline the numerous variations and the commonalities between cultures and allows you to make a decision for your self. When you travel you realise that many of the prejudices that you hold are incorrect and the only real way of finding out the truth when it comes to different cultural and social practices is to experience them first hand.

Ultimately, becoming cultured is something that you can do on an everyday basis; it's about questioning what you hear, questioning what you see, replying, whether that be through written work of your own or just through conversation. We've become a nation of people that sit in front of the TV every evening, watching television programs, however we don't really take them in, the screen could be blank but our expressions would be the same. It's time to stop that expression; it's time to start listening to what is being said and to start replying to culture around us. What would Harvey Specter do? Would he sit there all day watching daytime TV or would he get out there and experience the culture first hand? Whether that be music of various genres, art or various disciplines. Harvey is someone that is both cultured and somebody who constantly strives to culture himself further. To become Harvey Specter you need to start culturing yourself.

How To Date Beautiful Women

Lets be honest with ourselves, Harvey Specter gets all the good looking women and lets also be honest, that those good looking women these days, seem to possess the world. They've literally got the world by its balls. The reason for this is very simple, that's because very attractive women control the male population like panting puppets. Modern day society dictates that sex can be obtained when needed, whether it be through cash or other means, but the women are in control. Without lifting a finger, beautiful women could enjoy lives that some men could only fantasise about. Of course, before we go any further it's also worth making it clear that not all beautiful women decide to take this route. It's also quite possible for rather unattractive women to obtain a lavish lifestyle. For us men though, the lure of dating gorgeous women is because we want to be able to increase our social status among males; boost our own self-esteem. Perhaps even have a trophy wife. Harvey Specter likes dating beautiful women, simply because he likes beautiful things.

So, while all of this is fine gorgeous ladies also have their negative side and can sometimes be shallow, self centred, self-absorbed and can hold opinions that are selfish. Some of them believe their vaginas are gold-plated, some of them are manipulators and many of them hold many other negative characteristics. Just to clarify, plenty of men hold these same characteristics as well. But, despite these disadvantages, beautiful women are what most men search for and as these women are continually inundated with male attention, they're able to be highly selective when it comes to the people that they date. This often lands them with someone with money first and a visual appearance second; sometimes it's the other way around. The point is, they can be picky.

So, can there be any hope, without being a handsome man your self or holding lots of money? Well, I believe you still have a good shot. If you're willing to make a number of changes when it comes to your dating strategy and take my recommendations on dating gorgeous women.

The way to succeed when it comes to going on dates with beautiful women is different from going out with our friends. These ladies have heard everything so, if you want a serious chance of attracting these women you're going to need to make a different move. Here are some of the things you could do to make your self stand out-

Number 1

Treat her like she's nothing special. I don't mean disrespect her, but don't act awestruck by her looks. Don't repeatedly gush out compliments and stare at her with lustful eyes. Instead appear like it doesn't bother you, appear aloof.

Number 2

Discuss her interests and passions. So may men will sit in front of her and discuss what they've done, the amount of money that they earn, the car that they drive. Instead turn the conversation round and talk about her. Show curiosity about her intellect, making her comfortable.

Number 3

Don't compliment her. This might sound counter-intuitive, but don't put her on a pedestal where she usually sits along with other males. If you really need to compliment her, make it small and follow up with something off-putting. Let her know for example, that she's got nice shoes, but that your sister has got the same pair. This suggests that she has a good taste in fashion, however that she's not the first person to wear those shoes, therefore she's not entirely original.

Number 4

Wait. When you do get her number, don't phone straight away, wait a minimum of three days and when you do finally speak to her let her know that you'll try to fit something in; that your schedule is quite busy.

Number 5

Don't push for sex. Of course this is what you're after, but if you let her know that it's game over for you. She might put out, but it's safer to keep her guessing. Make her wait and it will drive her crazy.

Value Your Own Time

So once you have landed the dream job and turned your lifestyle into something that resembles Harvey Specter a little bit more, I feel you need to learn the very difficult skill of valuing your own time. This is something that so few of us do properly. When I say valuing your own time, I mean in a financial sense, but not just in a professional work environment.

I've been self-employed in the past and I may have valued my time at $80 and hour but in the sense of being self-employed, it's not really the freelancer that values your time it's the person that employs you. You're only worth what someone is willing to pay you. So, if you are able to achieve $80 an hour for your work, then you're worth $80 an hour. If you ask for $80 an hour and nobody accepts your proposals, your time isn't worth $80 an hour to them. So within a professional working environment it's quite easy to work out what your hourly rate is or how much someone values your time. Within your personal life though it gets a little bit trickier you can't just take that $80 an hour that your paid 9-5 into personal life and value your own time at $80 and hour. Heck, if you did that you would never do any of your own housework, you would never wash your own car and you would never do your own shopping because it would be cheaper to pay someone else to do it at $10 an hour.

The other odd thing about valuing your time outside of work is that it's not a fixed rate. You can't value your time at $40 an hour outside of work for the entire time because again if you did, you should never be picking up a mop and bucket and cleaning up. You shouldn't even cook your own food. In realty though, most people don't value their own personal time at all; they have a $0 value on it. What does that mean? Well, they see things like cleaners as an expense rather than a saving.

The best way to think about this is to analyse each job you do or each activity you take part in, in your personal life outside of work. So, when it comes to cleaning the house you might value your time at $5 an hour, I know I do. The reason for this is because- 1. I don't like it and 2. I'm rubbish at it. The better you are at something, the higher the value you should place on your own time and the more you enjoy the higher the value you should place on that time.

As an exercise, think what value you would place on ironing. Are you good at it? Can you whizz through a pile of 10 shirts in less than half an hour? Or do you groan every time you have to get the ironing board out? Work out a value or the task of ironing, then go and find some quotes from local launderette and see how much they charge per shirt or per hour for ironing. Valuing your own time allows you to enjoy your time outside of work more fully. It also helps you look at your own time ore constructively.

5 STYLE, STYLE, STYLE

"You don't send a puppy to clean up its own mess"

Want to know how to be more like Harvey Specter? Well, you're going to have to know how to wear a suit properly. The show is named after the very item of clothing that Harvey wears pretty much all the time. I won't bore you with the history of suits as a clothing item, however they do date back a long way. Today a suit is quite possibly the most stylish fashion statement a man can make. Yes, we like the scruffy flannel and jeans look, but when you need to look sharp, intelligent and wise, you cannot beat a suit. When worn correctly that is. Many blokes don't know how to wear a suit properly; they get nowhere near perfection when it comes to wearing a suit. The trousers end up being too long, the jacket sleeves are to short, the lapels are too wide or too skinny and the buttons are almost always too tight. I could go on, in fact I will; below I have outlined some of the most common mistakes men make when they put their suit on in the morning. Print this out, tear it out, laminate it and make sure you pay attention to it when you put your suit on the next time. And please after reading this, promise me that you'll never commit any of these errors again.

Error Number 1

Letting an undershirt poke through above the neckline of your main dress shirt. This is just really a no no. It makes you look like a bit of a schoolboy and it's also totally unnecessary. All you need to do is pop out to your local store and buy a little v-neck undershirt. You could of course go one better and not wear an undershirt at all. They are in no way needed.

Error Number 2

Not having your jacket sleeves customised. Most men think that once their trousers are hemmed to the right length, that's it done. But the jacket sleeves are just as important to get right. Too long and your suit makes you look careless, too short and your sleeves make you look dorky and stupid. Make certain that the jacket sleeves finish half an inch above your shirtsleeve. Additionally, make sure you tailor the jacket width round the bicep and also the torso. Most guys suit jackets are either, far too spacious which will make you look fat or far too tight which makes you look like an idiot.

Error Number 3

Selecting jackets which are too long. If you want a great way to test this, allow the jacket hem to fall to where the tips of your fingers finish naturally. It's as simple as that.

Error Number 4

Failing to get rid of the company label from the jacket sleeves. Why on earth do I care where your suit comes from, if it doesn't fit properly I'm not bothered and if it does, and I think it's a fine fitting suit then you've got no need to show me what shop you bought it from.

Error Number 5

Forgetting to cut the thread around the rear vent and also the pockets. This is something you forget to do when you're at school and when I say school, I mean kindergarten.

Error Number 6

Buying a suit with jacket lapels that are too big. If they look like they could be the wings of an aeroplane, they are too big. Three inches is a good guess for the widest your suit lapel should ever be. Equally though, don't go picking something with one centimetre lapels.

Error Number 7

Putting on trousers, which are too long. Watch out for the break, the break is where the fabric of the trousers touches your shoe and develops a horizontal crease, which is known as the break. Trousers without any break means that they are too short, as they don't even meet the shoe. Whilst this is trendy, it's not what Harvey would do and it won't be fashionable within a couple of years. Or at least I hope. Instead aim for a break of around an inch.

Error Number 8

Putting on trousers with cuffs. These are just not in fashion right now and when they do come back in fashion you should ignore them anyway.

Error Number 9

Selecting shirts, which are too big. You might see some weight lifters with bulging biceps whose shirts are extremely tight, but generally the problem most men have is purchasing a shirt that is too big. If you're stuck, stick to the one finger rule. That is, if you're able to fit several fingers between your collar and your neck, then it's too big. As for the torso, just buy a slim cut shirt. When it's billowing out and bunching at the sides it's just not a good look and it means its way too big.

Error Number 10

Thinking that suits can only be worn in block colours. First of all there's pinstripes. Pinstripes when done properly look great. Leave bold pin striping to Gordon Gecko, but a subtle print shouldn't go amiss on a couple of your suits. Also look into some plaid options or even a check.

Error Number 11

Only wearing black. Yes, Harvey does wear a lot of black suits but, you'll also notice he wears a lot of other colours as well. Black looks good, but wear it everyday and it looks quite boring.

Error Number 12

Wearing French cuffs which look like flippers. French cuffs or double cuffs worn with suitable cuff links can really add that va va voom to your suit. It can be especially handy in a more formal occasion. The problem comes when your cuffs are thirty centimetres long. Worse still is when they're too big around the wrist. They end up flapping around and make you look like an idiot.

Error Number 13

Letting your tie peak out from underneath the back and sides of your collar. If this happens then your collar is simply too small or your tie is too big. Either way, make sure that this never happens.

Error Number 14

Worrying about the expense of extras rather than the base model itself. Tie clips, French cuffs, cuff links these are all things that are gained, not merely given. You need to know how to rock a suit first. You need to know that the suit fits you properly and how to pick a shirt that compliments that suit. You need to know how to wear a suit as a professional first and then allow yourself to break those rules as an artist with tie clips and cuff links.

Effortless and Timeless Style Tips

Whilst Harvey Specter is a man that is normally wearing a suit, sometimes we see him out of one. We've already covered how to rock a suit in the same way that Harvey Specter does. Now its time to look at how we can replicate the rest of his wardrobe; for me, Harvey has and effortless and timeless style. He's never leading fashion trends, he's not even setting them or following them, he's doing his own thing at his own pace and in a way this style is the easiest to replicate. During this section of the book, I'll explore the idea of timeless style within men's fashion and have a look at the people who embody it.

First of all, timeless style is quite easy to define yet more complicated to explain simply. On a very basic level it is a look that will never go out of date, expire or become unfashionable. For me though, and I'm sure this goes for Harvey as well timeless style is more than just this. Like other areas of men's fashion and men's clothing, it's elusive.

Men don't have the same amount of preference and options within our wardrobe as women do. Just think for a moment, we could wear shorts or trousers, perhaps maybe a kilt if you're Scottish. Women have got shorts and trousers; they've also got skirts and dresses. As such, men compensate with rules and fashions on these traditional styles. Timeless and effortless fashion style though is usually just about putting on the clothes that embody you as a persona. People don't change; therefore if you match your clothing to yourself, your clothes and your clothing style will never change.

But how can one piece of clothing become timeless? Well most pieces of clothing at some stage, will become part of a trend. This is the cyclical character of the fashion industry that repeats trends from twenty years past. Timeless clothing therefore has to live through this. So its important to remember that timeless clothing can also be currently in fashion.

If we look at some of the people that embody this timeless style, there are a number of people that come to mind- Steve McQueen, James Dean, Otis Reading, Johnny Depp, Sammy Davis Jr, George Clooney, Tom Ford, Jamie Foxx, Douglass Booth and Alex Turner. These are all very different people and again that highlights the fact that timeless style is timeless to that person. Ultimately though, these people are awesome.

To go back to the idea of fashion versus style, it can be a very complicated debate. On the one hand fashion comes first and creates the styles that live on, or you could argue that it's from existing styles that new fashions are created. It's the chicken and egg problem. Yves Saint Laurent famously said fashion is temporary, style is eternal but without these trends nothing would be given the opportunity to be categorised as stylish. I'm not here to judge whether dressing trendy or stylish is right; for me Harvey Specter is a man of style, so lets take a look at some of those effortlessly stylish items of clothing that he wears.

Leather Jackets

If we look back in history we see James Dean in a leather jacket, John Travolta in Grease, Arnold Swarzenegger in most of the Terminator films and loads of other examples of men in popular culture in different eras wearing leather jackets. The leather jacket is a style staple and Harvey Specter is a man that owns more than one of these. You can wear it with almost anything casual and most importantly its understated. Understated is a word that can be used time and time again when were looking at timeless styles.

The Duster Coat

It is an essential when it comes to spring time but you can wear it throughout the year and the duster coat hasn't gone in and out of fashion. Look back to films in the 1940's all the way up to the present day and the duster coat remains on screen. It's an absolute must-have piece of clothing. Whilst Harvey prefers the classic khaki colour you can get away with something a bit sharper. It's also something you can wear over your suit, but also over some simple jeans and a polo shirt combination. Put it on closed and tied for a more formal look or open the belt up and tie it around the back for a more casual appearance.

Polo shirt

The polo shirt is the love child of the dress shirt and the t-shirt, it tiptoes along the lines of smart and casual and blurs the boundaries so much so that now you'll find people turning up to work in a polo shirt, but equally going out on an evening in one with their friends. For this reason I love polo shirts and Harvey does too. They're versatile and can be used in almost every situation required. Best bet with these is to avoid the designs though and stick to plain block colours. Pair them up with some understated jeans or chinos and you've got a look that will get you into most restaurants in the world but you wouldn't look out of place watching a football match.

Jeans

Jeans used to be the workman's choice of trousers and whilst you wouldn't wear them in the workplace, or whilst you might not wear them in the workplace, they're a wardrobe staple that almost every man already possesses. The problem is most of these don't fit properly. You don't want to go for a straight leg cut, you need a slightly slimmer leg cut jean, just like you do when it comes to suits. My advice would be to buy one set of top end; dark indigo jeans in a slim cut and treat these as your best friends. When Harvey's not in a suit you'll generally find him in a set of dark indigo, slim jeans. Just like the polo shirt, this cut and colour of jean would get you into most places you need to go as well.

So there you have it, there's my advice on effortless and timeless style. Of course the great thing about purchasing these items as well, is that you only need to replace them when they're worn out, not when they go out of fashion. How often have you found yourself, with a t-shirt with a dragon on thinking that, that would be a great look. After three days you realise the trend has moved on and you're left with a t-shirt with a dragon on. Who wants a t-shirt with a dragon on, certainly not Harvey? Stick to timeless and effortless style; you'll end up saving money, looking great and looking more and more like Harvey Specter every day.

6 WORDS OF WARNING

"I refuse to answer that on the grounds that I don't want to."

Don't be a douchebag. Harvey is a wealthy man, he has lots of female company, he has a great job, he drives great cars and he parties like a rock star. However, he is not a douchebag. In this final section of the book, I will tell you how to not be a douchebag on your quest to become more and more like Harvey Specter.

Cast your mind back to the 1990's, Mel Gibson was finishing one of his greatest films to date. Now think back to where we are today, he's one of the greatest douchebags in the world. But it's not just Mel Gibson who's fallen foul and become a bit of a douche; many people are douchebags and many of them we interact with on a basic level everyday. They're on the T.V, on the radio, even working in McDonalds. So, when you're surrounded by douchebags, how do you go about protecting yourself from becoming one? It is a lot easier to prevent yourself from a becoming a douchebag than changing once you become one. So, here are my ten rules to avoid being a douchebag:

Rule Number 1

Pay your debts. Are you the bloke that keeps getting to the bar and having to ask for $20 from your friends, even though you probably already owe them $20? Are you the kind of person that makes out that you don't have much money to pay them back yet still ventures out that evening for a McDonalds? You are a douchebag! Pay your debts, especially if you owe your friends and family. For god sake, these are your friends and family and you're draining them of cash just so you can purchase the latest game.

Rule Number 2

Stop bragging. If you have an expensive car, people can see that. If you live in a nice house, people will recognise that and if you currently date a supermodel, almost everyone will know about it and that's without you telling them. Telling them about these things even once is like repeating it again and again and again. Rubbing peoples face in what you've got and what they haven't got. Life isn't fair we know that, but there's no need to rub salt in the wounds. People aren't blind and they know that you're living the good life already, so by telling them again you're only causing them pain. Quit bragging and stop being a douchebag.

Rule Number 3

Don't get jealous. Stop being flirty and excessively friendly with your best mates girlfriend. Leave her alone as she is not yours, although your best mate is not her maker either. Furthermore, if she's got a ring on her finger, leave her alone. The whole idea of the unattainable challenge is old, it's what you did when your high school. Instead, get out there and find your own single girl.

Rule Number 4

Stay attached. If you're married, you are married, stop looking around at every attractive woman that you walk past in the street. If you'd rather have plenty of promiscuous encounters then don't get married in the first place. Or, if you are, express your feelings and make sure everyone is clear with the situation. And in case you're thinking you just don't want to hurt her, that is not a good excuse and you are an enormous douchebag! Grow some balls and end it there, or just don't get into the relationship in the first place.

Rule Number 5

If you've got nothing nice to say, don't say nothing at

all. That's a line from a Disney film. Disney was trying to teach you how to not be a douchebag. If you're the kind of person who tells racist, sexist or violent jokes because you think they're funny; you are a douchebag. Luckily this is quite easily resolved. It's a two-step process that requires no medical assistance. The first step requires you to locate your mouth. The second step requires you to shut it. There is no third step. Should you encounter a third step, or should you find yourself opening your mouth again and spewing more offensive jokes; you have become a douchebag again.

Rule Number 6

Pay attention. Are you the kind of person that switches off halfway through a conversation? You nod away, agreeing and umming and arring, but then when it gets to the end of the conversation you haven't got a clue what they're talking about. If that's you, that could be the start of becoming a douchebag. If you're having a conversation with someone, listen to them. If you're not interested in the conversation, tell them that. Of course don't do this in a douchebag way.

Rule Number 7

Stick to what you say. Are you the kind of person that says, I'm going to do this; I'm going to do that that you never end up actually doing? Get rid of those empty promises because that's all they are. Your friends and family and everyone around you will begin to see you as the empty promise man. The empty promise man is a douchebag. The worst type of douchebag is the one that then proclaims that you have my word. A douchebags word is worth nothing.

Rule Number 8

Slow down. Are you the kind of person that insists everybody does shots at the start of the night, the middle of the night and the end of the night? Are you the kind of person that would accept any dare? "Jumping off a building, I'll take that". Even when some of those dares are just in jest. Do you constantly wake up wondering, "Did I really do that?" Or even worse, "what did I actually do?" If you're sat there like a nodding dog while trying to suppress embarrassed laughter, then you're not only a douchebag, but you are also an idiot. You are the bloke that everyone is poking fun at. Stop doing this. Here's some very brief suggestions- Drink less, think and get rid of the "I don't give a fuck" attitude. Since you should give a fuck. At the end of the day it's your personality and status that gets a bad name.

Rule Number 9

Care. If someone comes to you because their cat has just died, give them some time. To you it may seem stupid that Mr. Jiggles has passed away and that your neighbour id weeping uncontrollably at your door now. To you it might be the most annoying cat in the world; to them though it was their pet, it was their friend. Have a bit of sympathy, have a bit of empathy and give a hug to those who need it.

Rule Number 10

It isn't about you. When you're having a shit day, do you feel like the world is aligning to piss you off? When you're having a great day are you the first to everyone about it? Well let's get one thing straight; this world is not about you. It's not about anyone in particular. There are over 7 billion people on this planet and if we all though like that it would be a pretty shit place to live. The planet was not produced for your enjoyment, everyone on this planet is not a puppet that you control. If you think like this, you are a douchebag.

Whilst this section and in fact this whole book was a light-hearted look at how to become the character Harvey Specter; I feel it is very important to highlight the fact that Harvey Specter isn't a douchebag. If you're aiming to become him do not become a douchebag instead, this world has enough of those already, we don't need another one.

ABOUT THE AUTHOR

"It's not bragging if it's true"

Lee Burr works within the legal sector in both the UK and USA. Needless to say, it is not his real name.